2010 SUPPLEMENT

CONSTITUTIONAL LAW

SEVENTEENTH EDITION

by

KATHLEEN M. SULLIVAN
Stanley Morrison Professor of Law and
Former Dean of the School of Law,
Stanford University

GERALD GUNTHER
Late William Nelson Cromwell Professor of Law Emeritus,
Stanford University

FOUNDATION PRESS
2010

THOMSON REUTERS

© 2010 By THOMSON REUTERS/FOUNDATION PRESS

1 New York Plaza, 34th Floor

New York, NY 10004

Phone Toll Free 1–877–888–1330

Fax (646) 424–5201

foundation–press.com

Printed in the United States of America

ISBN 978–1–59941–821–6

Mat #40979999

TABLE OF CONTENTS

Page numbers on the left indicate where the new cases fit into the casebook. Principal cases are in **bold face**.

TABLE OF CASES

Principal cases are in bold type. Non-principal cases are in roman type. References are to Pages.

TABLE OF AUTHORITIES

References are to Pages.

2010 SUPPLEMENT

CONSTITUTIONAL LAW

CHAPTER 3

THE COMMERCE CLAUSE AND ITS FEDERALISM–BASED LIMITS

SECTION 4. THE REHNQUIST COURT'S REVIVAL OF INTERNAL LIMITS ON THE COMMERCE CLAUSE

Page 126. Add after note 4:

5. *Federalism-based limits on the Necessary and Proper Clause?* Recall that in McCulloch v. Maryland (1819; 17th ed. p. 63), the Supreme Court read the Necessary and Proper Clause of Article I, § 8, cl. 18, broadly in support of Congress's power to charter a national bank. Do the federalism-based limits on the commerce power developed in the line of cases from Lopez to Raich have any application to the Necessary and Proper Clause? In UNITED STATES v. COMSTOCK, ___ U.S. ___, 130 S.Ct. 1949 (2010), the Court considered the question whether the Necessary and Proper Clause grants authority to Congress to enact a statute, 18 U.S.C. § 4248, allowing federal district courts to order the civil commitment of mentally ill, sexually dangerous federal prisoners beyond the dates they would otherwise be released. The Court found, by a vote of 7–2, that the Clause does grant such authority. Justice BREYER wrote for the Court, joined by Chief Justice Roberts and Justices Stevens, Ginsburg and Sotomayor: "Here we ask whether the Federal Government has the authority under Article I of the Constitution to enact this federal civil-commitment program or whether its doing so falls beyond the reach of a government 'of enumerated powers.' McCulloch v. Maryland. [We] conclude that the Constitution grants Congress legislative power sufficient to enact § 4248. We base this conclusion on five considerations, taken together.

"First, the Necessary and Proper Clause grants Congress broad authority to enact federal legislation [that is] 'convenient, or useful' or 'conducive' to the authority's 'beneficial exercise.' [McCulloch.] Neither Congress' power to criminalize conduct, nor its power to imprison individuals who engage in that conduct, nor its power to enact laws governing prisons and prisoners, is explicitly mentioned in the Constitution. But Congress nonetheless possesses broad authority to do each of those things in the course of 'carrying into Execution' [its] enumerated powers. Second, the civil-commitment statute before us constitutes a modest addition to a set of federal prison-related mental-health statutes that have existed [since] 1855. Third, Congress reasonably extended its longstanding civil-commitment system to cover mentally ill and sexually dangerous persons who are already in federal custody, even if doing so detains them beyond the termination of their criminal sentence. [The] Federal Government is the custodian of its prisoners [and] has the constitutional power to act in order to protect nearby (and other) communities from the

1

danger federal prisoners may pose. [Moreover,] § 4248 is 'reasonably adapted' to Congress' power to act as a responsible federal custodian. Congress could have reasonably concluded that federal inmates who suffer from a mental illness that causes them to 'have serious difficulty in refraining from sexually violent conduct' would pose an especially high danger to the public if released. And Congress could also have reasonably concluded [that] a reasonable number of such individuals would likely not be detained by the States if released from federal custody. Fourth, the statute properly accounts for state interests. [Section 4248 does not] invade state sovereignty [but rather] requires accommodation of state interests: [it] requires the Attorney General to encourage the relevant States to take custody of the individual without inquiring into the 'suitability' of their intended care or treatment, and to relinquish federal authority whenever a State asserts its own. Fifth, the links between § 4248 and an enumerated Article I power are not too attenuated. [We need not] fear that our holding today confers on Congress a general 'police power' [for] § 4248 is narrow in scope. It has been applied to only a small fraction of federal prisoners. And its reach is limited to individuals already 'in the custody of the' Federal Government. [Taken] together, these considerations lead us to conclude that the statute is a 'necessary and proper' means of exercising the federal authority that permits Congress to create federal criminal laws, to punish their violation, to imprison violators, to provide appropriately for those imprisoned, and to maintain the security of those who are not imprisoned but who may be affected by the federal imprisonment of others.''

Justice KENNEDY, joined by Justice Alito, filed a concurrence in the judgment, agreeing that § 4248 was a necessary and proper exercise of congressional authority, but emphasizing that the rationality review applicable to a Necessary and Proper Clause inquiry should not be as deferential as the minimal rationality test employed in due process inquiries: "[U]nder the Necessary and Proper Clause, application of a 'rational basis' test should be at least as exacting as it has been in the Commerce Clause cases, if not more so. [Those] precedents require a tangible link to commerce, not a mere conceivable rational relation, as in [the due process cases]. The rational basis referred to in the Commerce Clause context is a demonstrated link in fact, based on empirical demonstration."

Justice ALITO filed a separate concurrence in the judgment, opining that it is "necessary and proper for Congress to protect the public from dangers created by the federal criminal justice and prison systems. [Just] as it is necessary and proper for Congress to provide for the apprehension of escaped federal prisoners, it is necessary and proper for Congress to provide for the civil commitment of dangerous federal prisoners who would otherwise escape civil commitment as a result of federal imprisonment."

Justice THOMAS, joined for the most part by Justice Scalia, filed a dissent objecting that the statute intrudes too far upon the authority of the States: "§ 4248 can be a valid exercise of congressional authority only if it is 'necessary and proper for carrying into Execution' one or more of those federal powers actually enumerated in the Constitution. [The] Government identifies no specific enumerated power or powers as a constitutional predicate for § 4248, and none are readily discernable. Indeed, not even the Commerce Clause [can] justify federal civil detention of sex offenders [as sexual violence is a noneconomic activity]. [The] power to care for the mentally ill and, where necessary, the power 'to protect the community from the dangerous tendencies of some' mentally ill persons, are among the numerous powers that remain with the States. [True,] 29 States appear as amici and argue that § 4248 is constitutional. They tell us that they do not object to Congress retaining custody of 'sexually dangerous persons' after their criminal sentences expire because the cost of detaining such persons is 'expensive' [and] these States would rather the Federal Government bear this expense. Congress' power, however, is fixed by the Constitution; it does not expand merely to suit the States' policy preferences, or to allow State officials to avoid difficult choices regarding the allocation of state funds. [Today's] opinion [comes] perilously close to transforming the Necessary and Proper Clause into a basis for [a] federal police power.''

CHAPTER 6

SEPARATION OF POWERS

SECTION 3. CONGRESSIONAL VIOLATION OF THE SEPARATION OF POWERS

Page 321. Add to the end of note 3:

The principles set forth in Myers and Humphrey's Executor governing limits on the executive removal power were explored again in FREE ENTERPRISE FUND v. PUBLIC COMPANY ACCOUNTING OVERSIGHT BOARD, ___ U.S. ___, 130 S.Ct. 3138 (2010). Established as part of a series of accounting reforms in the Sarbanes–Oxley Act of 2002, the Public Company Accounting Oversight Board is composed of five members appointed by the Securities and Exchange Commission (SEC), which is required by statute to be bipartisan. The Board has broad authority to inspect and investigate private accounting firms and impose sanctions against them. The SEC may remove Board members only for "good cause," and the President may remove SEC Commissioners only for "inefficiency, neglect of duty, or malfeasance in office."

In a 5–4 decision invalidating the removal provision as violating the separation of powers, Chief Justice ROBERTS wrote for the Court, joined by Justices Scalia, Kennedy, Thomas, and Alito: "We have previously [e.g., in Humphrey's Executor and Morrison v. Olson (1988; 17th ed. p. 322)] upheld limited restrictions on the President's removal power. In those cases, however, only one level of protected tenure separated the President from an officer exercising executive power. It was the President—or a subordinate he could remove at will—who decided whether the officer's conduct merited removal under the good-cause standard. The Act before us does something quite different. It not only protects Board members from removal except for good cause, but withdraws from the President any decision on whether that good cause exists. That decision is vested instead in other tenured officers—the Commissioners—none of whom is subject to the President's direct control. The result is a Board that is not accountable to the President, and a President who is not responsible for the Board.

"The added layer of tenure protection makes a difference. Without a layer of insulation between the Commission and the Board, the Commission could remove a Board member at any time, and therefore would be fully responsible for what the Board does. The President could then hold the Commission to account for its supervision of the Board, to the same extent that he may hold the Commission to account for everything else it does. A second level of tenure protection changes the nature of the President's review. Now the Commission cannot remove a Board member at will. The President therefore cannot hold the Commission fully accountable for the Board's conduct, to the same extent that he may hold the Commission accountable for everything else that it does.

The Commissioners are not responsible for the Board's actions. They are only responsible for their own determination of whether the Act's rigorous good-cause standard is met. And even if the President disagrees with their determination, he is powerless to intervene—unless that determination is so unreasonable as to constitute 'inefficiency, neglect of duty, or malfeasance in office.' This novel structure does not merely add to the Board's independence, but transforms it. Neither the President, nor anyone directly responsible to him, nor even an officer whose conduct he may review only for good cause, has full control over the Board. The President is stripped of the power our precedents have preserved, and his ability to execute the laws—by holding his subordinates accountable for their conduct—is impaired. That arrangement is contrary to Article II's vesting of the executive power in the President." The majority found the invalid removal provisions severable, excising them and leaving Board members removable by the SEC at will while leaving the rest of Sarbanes–Oxley intact.

Justice BREYER filed a dissent joined by Justices Stevens, Ginsburg and Sotomayor: "In Myers, the Court invalidated—for the first and only time—a congressional statute on the ground that it unduly limited the President's authority to remove an Executive Branch official. But soon thereafter the Court expressly disapproved most of Myers' broad reasoning. See Humphrey's Executor. [The] Court has since said that 'the essence of the decision in Myers' [was] the judgment that the Constitution prevents Congress from 'draw[ing] to itself ... the power to remove or the right to participate in the exercise of that power.' Morrison. [Congress] has not granted itself any role in removing the members of the Accounting Board. [When] previously deciding this kind of nontextual question, the Court has emphasized the importance of examining how a particular provision, taken in context, is likely to function. [E.g., Steel Seizure.] It is not surprising that the Court in these circumstances has looked to function and context, and not to bright-line rules. For one thing, that approach embodies the intent of the Framers. As Chief Justice Marshall long ago observed, our Constitution is fashioned so as to allow the three coordinate branches, including this Court, to exercise practical judgment in response to changing conditions and 'exigencies.' McCulloch. For another, a functional approach permits Congress and the President the flexibility needed to adapt statutory law to changing circumstances.

"[The] 'for cause' restriction before us will not restrict presidential power significantly. For one thing, the restriction directly limits, not the President's power, but the power of an already independent agency. [The] statute provides the Commission with full authority and virtually comprehensive control over all of the Board's functions. [The] Commission's control over the Board's investigatory and legal functions is virtually absolute. Moreover, the Commission [controls] the Board's budget, [can] assign to the Board any 'duties or functions' that it 'determines are necessary or appropriate,' [and] has full 'oversight and enforcement authority over the Board,' including the authority to inspect the Board's activities whenever it believes it 'appropriate' to do so. [Everyone] concedes that the President's control over the Commission is constitutionally sufficient. See Humphrey's Executor. And if the President's control over the Commission is sufficient, and the Commission's control over the Board is virtually absolute, then, as a practical matter, the President's control over the Board should prove sufficient as well. [This] Court has long recognized the

appropriateness of using 'for cause' provisions to protect the personal independence of those who [engage] in adjudicatory functions. Humphrey's Executor.
Moreover, in addition to their adjudicative functions, the Accounting Board
members supervise, and are themselves, technical professional experts. This
Court has recognized [the] constitutional legitimacy of a justification that rests
agency independence upon the need for technical expertise. Humphrey's Executor. [Congress] and the President could reasonably have thought it prudent to
insulate the adjudicative Board members from fear of purely politically based
removal.''

CHAPTER 7

THE BILL OF RIGHTS AND THE POST–CIVIL WAR AMENDMENTS

SECTION 3. THE "INCORPORATION" OF THE BILL OF RIGHTS THROUGH THE DUE PROCESS CLAUSE

Page 374. Add to the end of Note 4:

While Heller explicitly refrained from opining on whether the Second Amendment applies to the States, the Court reached that question in McDONALD v. CITY OF CHICAGO, ___ U.S. ___, 130 S.Ct. 3020 (2010), answering in the affirmative. The case involved municipal handgun registration ordinances that effectively banned almost all private handgun possession by private residents of the cities of Chicago and Oak Park, Illinois. Justice ALITO wrote for the Court, speaking for a plurality joined by Chief Justice Roberts and Justices Scalia and Kennedy for the proposition that the Second Amendment right to individual gun ownership is incorporated against the States by the Due Process Clause of the Fourteenth Amendment. Justice Thomas concurred in part and in the judgment on the alternative ground that the right is extended against the States by the Privileges or Immunities Clause of that Amendment.

In the due process incorporation discussion, Justice Alito wrote (here speaking for the Court): "[In answering] the question whether the Second Amendment right to keep and bear arms is incorporated in the concept of due process, [we] must decide whether the right to keep and bear arms is fundamental to our scheme of ordered liberty, Duncan, or [whether] this right is 'deeply rooted in this Nation's history and tradition.' [Our] decision in Heller points unmistakably to the answer. Self-defense is a basic right, recognized by many legal systems from ancient times to the present day, and in Heller, we held that individual self-defense is 'the central component' of the Second Amendment right. Explaining that the need for defense of self, family, and property is most acute in the home, we found that this right applies to handguns because they are 'the most preferred firearm in the nation to "keep" and use for protection of one's home and family.' Thus, we concluded, citizens must be permitted 'to use [handguns] for the core lawful purpose of self-defense.' Heller makes it clear that this right is 'deeply rooted in this Nation's history and tradition.' Heller explored the right's origins, noting that the 1689 English Bill of Rights explicitly protected a right to keep arms for self-defense, and that by 1765, Blackstone was able to assert that the right to keep and bear arms was 'one of the fundamental rights of Englishmen.' Blackstone's assessment was shared by the American colonists. As we noted in Heller, King George III's attempt to disarm the colonists in the 1760's and 1770's 'provoked polemical reactions by Americans invoking their rights as Englishmen to keep arms.'

"The right to keep and bear arms was considered no less fundamental by those who drafted and ratified the Bill of Rights. 'During the 1788 ratification debates, the fear that the federal government would disarm the people in order to impose rule through a standing army or select militia was pervasive in Antifederalist rhetoric.' Heller. Federalists responded, not by arguing that the right was insufficiently important to warrant protection but by contending that the right was adequately protected by the Constitution's assignment of only limited powers to the Federal Government. Thus, Antifederalists and Federalists alike agreed that the right to bear arms was fundamental to the newly formed system of government. But those who were fearful that the new Federal Government would infringe traditional rights such as the right to keep and bear arms insisted on the adoption of the Bill of Rights as a condition for ratification of the Constitution. This is surely powerful evidence that the right was regarded as fundamental in the sense relevant here. This understanding persisted in the years immediately following the ratification of the Bill of Rights. In addition to the four States that had adopted Second Amendment analogues before ratification, nine more States adopted state constitutional provisions protecting an individual right to keep and bear arms between 1789 and 1820. Founding-era legal commentators confirmed the importance of the right to early Americans. [See] 3 J. Story, Commentaries on the Constitution of the United States § 1890, p. 746 (1833) ('The right of the citizens to keep and bear arms has justly been considered, as the palladium of the liberties of a republic; since it offers a strong moral check against the usurpation and arbitrary power of rulers; and will generally, even if these are successful in the first instance, enable the people to resist and triumph over them.')."

Reviewing the post-Civil war context in which the Fourteenth Amendment was enacted, Justice Alito continued (still speaking for the Court): "After the Civil War, many of the over 180,000 African Americans who served in the Union Army returned to the States of the old Confederacy, where systematic efforts were made to disarm them and other blacks. The laws of some States formally prohibited African Americans from possessing firearms. [Throughout] the South, armed parties, often consisting of ex-Confederate soldiers serving in the state militias, forcibly took firearms from newly freed slaves." Justice Alito noted that both the Freedmen's Bureau Act and the Civil Rights Act of 1866 expressly protected the right to bear arms without regard to race, but that the 39th Congress deemed such legislative remedies insufficient and, "[i]n debating the Fourteenth Amendment, [referred] to the right to keep and bear arms as a fundamental right deserving of protection." Rejecting the city respondents' argument that the Framers of the Fourteenth Amendment intended to bar only racially discriminatory gun laws, he stated, "It cannot be doubted that the right to bear arms was regarded as a substantive guarantee, not a prohibition that could be ignored so long as the States legislated in an evenhanded manner."

Speaking only for the plurality, Justice Alito concluded by rejecting, as "inconsistent with the long-established standard we apply in incorporation cases," the city respondents' argument that "the Due Process Clause protects only those rights 'recognized by all temperate and civilized governments, from a deep and universal sense of [their] justice,'" an argument he interpreted to hold that, "if it is possible to imagine *any* civilized legal system that does not recognize a particular right, then the Due Process Clause does not make that right binding on the States." He thus dismissed the cities' argument that, because such nations as "England, Canada, Australia, Japan, Denmark, Finland, Luxembourg, and New Zealand either ban or severely limit handgun ownership, it must follow that no right to possess such weapons is protected by the Fourteenth Amendment." He continued: "We likewise reject municipal respondents' argument that we should depart from our established incorporation methodology on the ground that making the Second Amendment binding on the States and their subdivisions is inconsistent with principles of federalism and will stifle experimentation." He concluded: "In Heller, we held that the Second Amendment protects the right to possess a handgun in the home for the purpose of self-defense. Unless considerations of stare decisis counsel otherwise, a provision of the Bill of Rights that protects a right that is fundamental from an American perspective applies equally to the Federal Government and the States. We therefore hold that the Due Process Clause of the Fourteenth Amendment incorporates the Second Amendment right recognized in Heller."

Justice SCALIA concurred, joining the Court's opinion "[d]espite my misgivings about Substantive Due Process as an original matter": "I have acquiesced in the Court's incorporation of certain guarantees in the Bill of Rights 'because it is both long established and narrowly limited.' This case does not require me to reconsider that view, since straightforward application of settled doctrine suffices to decide it."

Justice THOMAS filed a partial concurrence and concurrence in the judgment, arguing that the Privileges or Immunities rather than the Due Process Clause is the appropriate vehicle for incorporating the Second Amendment right against the States: "Applying what is now a well-settled test, the plurality opinion concludes that the right to keep and bear arms applies to the States through the Fourteenth Amendment's Due Process Clause because it is 'fundamental' to the American 'scheme of ordered liberty,' and 'deeply rooted in this Nation's history and tradition.' I agree with that description of the right. But I cannot agree that it is enforceable against the States through a clause that speaks only to 'process.' Instead, the right to keep and bear arms is a privilege of American citizenship that applies to the States through the Fourteenth Amendment's Privileges or Immunities Clause."

Justice Thomas acknowledged that the Court's precedents had defined the privileges or immunities of national citizenship "narrowly," noting that the Slaughter–House Cases had "defined that category to include only those rights 'which owe their existence to the Federal government, its National character, its Constitution, or its laws,'" and that later cases had "interpret[ed] the Privileges or Immunities Clause even more narrowly": "Chief among those cases is United States v. Cruikshank, 92 U.S. 542 (1876). There, the Court held that members of a white militia who had brutally murdered as many as 165 black Louisianians congregating outside a courthouse had not deprived the victims of their privileges as American citizens to peaceably assemble or to keep and bear arms. According to the Court, the right to peaceably assemble codified in the First Amendment was not a privilege of United States citizenship because '[t]he right ... existed long before the adoption of the Constitution.' Similarly, the Court held that the right to keep and bear arms was not a privilege of United States citizenship because it was not 'in any manner dependent upon that instrument for its existence.'" After an exhaustive review of the contemporaneous history and legislative history surrounding enactment of the Fourteenth Amendment, he concluded: "This history confirms what the text of the Privileges or Immunities Clause most naturally suggests: Consistent with its command that '[n]o State shall ... abridge' the rights of United States citizens, the Clause establishes a minimum baseline of federal rights, and the constitutional right to keep and bear arms plainly was among them."

Justice Thomas rejected the view that stare decisis compels deference to The Slaughter–House Cases' interpretation of "the rights of state and federal citizenship as mutually exclusive": "The better view, in light of the States and Federal Government's shared history of recognizing certain inalienable rights in their citizens, is that the privileges and immunities of state and federal citizenship overlap. [A] separate question is whether the privileges and immunities of American citizenship include any rights besides those enumerated in the Constitution. [Because] this case does not involve an unenumerated right, it is not necessary to resolve the question whether the Clause protects such rights." Finally, Justice Thomas argued, Cruikshank, which "squarely held that the right to keep and bear arms was not a privilege of American citizenship, thereby overturning the convictions of militia members responsible for the brutal Colfax Massacre, [is] not a precedent entitled to any respect": "Cruikshank's holding that blacks could look only to state governments for protection of their right to keep and bear arms enabled private forces, often with the assistance of local governments, to subjugate the newly freed slaves and their descendants through a wave of private violence designed to drive blacks from the voting booth and force them into peonage, an effective return to slavery. Without federal enforcement of the inalienable right to keep and bear arms, these militias and mobs were tragically successful in waging a campaign of terror against the very people the Fourteenth Amendment had just made citizens." Justice Thomas concluded: "I agree with the Court that the Second Amendment is fully applicable to the States. I do so because the right to keep and bear arms is guaranteed by the Fourteenth Amendment as a privilege of American citizenship."

Justice STEVENS filed an exhaustive, solo dissent stating "[t]his is a substantive due process case." In an extended discussion of substantive due process methodology, he stressed that interpretation of the Due Process Clause should not be too rigidly historical: "The Court hinges its entire decision on one mode of intellectual history, culling selected pronouncements and enactments from the 18th and 19th centuries to ascertain what Americans thought about firearms. [The] plurality suggests that only interests that have proved 'fundamental from an American perspective,' or 'deeply rooted in this Nation's history and tradition,' to the Court's satisfaction, may qualify for incorporation into the Fourteenth Amendment. To the extent the Court's opinion could be read to imply that the historical pedigree of a right is the exclusive or dispositive determinant of its status under the Due Process Clause, the opinion is seriously mistaken." At the same time, he emphasized the need for judicial modesty and self-restraint in substantive due process interpretation, stating that "it is incumbent upon us, as federal judges contemplating a novel rule that would bind all 50 States, to proceed cautiously and to decide only what must be decided."

Having laid out general interpretive principles, Justice Stevens continued: "Understood as a plea to keep their preferred type of firearm in the home, petitioners' argument has real force. The decision to keep a loaded handgun in the house is often motivated by the desire to protect life, liberty, and property. It is comparable, in some ways, to decisions about the education and upbringing of one's children. For it is the kind of decision that may have profound consequences for every member of the family, and for the world beyond. [Bolstering] petitioners' claim, our law has long recognized that the home provides a kind of special sanctuary in modern life. [The] State generally has a lesser basis for regulating private as compared to public acts, and firearms kept inside the home generally pose a lesser threat to public welfare as compared to firearms taken outside."

He concluded, however, that, "[w]hile I agree with the Court that our substantive due process cases offer a principled basis for holding that petitioners have a constitutional right to possess a usable firearm in the home, I am ultimately persuaded that a better reading of our case law supports the city of Chicago. I would not foreclose the possibility that a particular plaintiff—say, an elderly widow who lives in a dangerous neighborhood and does not have the strength to operate a long gun—may have a cognizable liberty interest in possessing a handgun. But I cannot accept petitioners' broader submission. A number of factors, taken together, lead me to this conclusion.

"First, firearms have a fundamentally ambivalent relationship to liberty. Just as they can help homeowners defend their families and property from intruders, they can help thugs and insurrectionists murder innocent victims. The threat that firearms will be misused is far from hypothetical, for gun crime has devastated many of our communities. [Second,] the right to possess a firearm of one's choosing is different in kind from the liberty interests we have recognized under the Due Process Clause. [It] does not appear to be the case that the ability to own a handgun, or any particular type of firearm, is critical to leading a life of autonomy, dignity, or political equality. [Third,] the experience of other advanced democracies, including those that share our British heritage, undercuts the notion that an expansive right to keep and bear arms is intrinsic to ordered liberty. Many of these countries place restrictions on the possession, use, and carriage of firearms far more onerous than the restrictions found in this Nation. [Fourth,] the Second Amendment differs in kind from the Amendments that surround it, [in that it] was the States, not private persons, on whose immediate behalf the Second Amendment was adopted. Notwithstanding [Heller's] efforts to write the Second Amendment's preamble out of the Constitution, the Amendment still serves the structural function of protecting the States from encroachment by an overreaching Federal Government. [Fifth,] although it may be true that Americans' interest in firearm possession and state-law recognition of that interest are 'deeply rooted' in some important senses, it is equally true that the States have a long and unbroken history of regulating firearms. [Finally, this] is a quintessential area in which federalism ought to be allowed to flourish without this Court's meddling. [States] and localities vary significantly in the patterns and problems of gun violence they face, as well as in the traditions and cultures of lawful gun use they claim. The city of Chicago, for example, faces a pressing challenge in combating criminal street gangs. Most rural areas do not."

Justice BREYER, joined by Justices Ginsburg and Sotomayor, filed a separate dissent. Noting that Justice Stevens's dissent focused on substantive due process concerns, Justice Breyer wrote to "separately consider the question of 'incorporation,'" stating that "I can find nothing in the Second Amendment's text, history, or underlying rationale that could warrant characterizing it as 'fundamental' insofar as it seeks to protect the keeping and bearing of arms for private self-defense purposes. [The] majority here [relies] almost exclusively upon history to make the necessary showing. But to do so for incorporation purposes is both wrong and dangerous. [Where] history provides no clear answer, [it is proper] to look to other factors in considering whether a right is sufficiently 'fundamental' to remove it from the political process in every State. I would include among those factors the nature of the right; any contemporary disagreement about whether the right is fundamental; the extent to which incorporation will further other, perhaps more basic, constitutional aims; and the extent to which incorporation will advance or hinder the Constitution's structural aims, including its division of powers among different governmental institutions (and the people as well). Is incorporation needed, for example, to further the Constitution's effort to ensure that the government treats each individual with equal respect? Will it help maintain the democratic form of government that the Constitution foresees?

"[How] do these considerations apply here? [There] is no popular consensus that the private self-defense right described in Heller is fundamental. [One] side believes the right essential to protect the lives of those attacked in the home; the other side believes it essential to regulate the right in order to protect the lives of others attacked with guns. It seems unlikely that definitive evidence will develop one way or the other. [Moreover,] there is no reason here to believe that incorporation of the private self-defense right will further any other or broader constitutional objective. We are aware of no argument that gun-control regulations target or are passed with the purpose of targeting 'discrete and insular minorities.' Carolene Products. Nor will incorporation help to assure equal respect for individuals. Unlike the First Amendment's rights of free speech, free press, assembly, and petition, the private self-defense right does not comprise a necessary part of the democratic process that the Constitution seeks to establish. Unlike the First Amendment's religious protections, the Fourth Amendment's protection against unreasonable searches and seizures, the Fifth and Sixth Amendments' insistence upon fair criminal procedure, and the Eighth Amendment's protection against cruel and unusual punishments, the private self-defense right does not significantly seek to protect individuals who might otherwise suffer unfair or inhumane treatment at the hands of a majority. Unlike the protections offered by many of these same Amendments, it does not involve matters as to which judges possess a comparative expertise, by virtue of their close familiarity with the justice system and its operation.

"[Finally,] incorporation of the right will work a significant disruption in the constitutional allocation of decisionmaking authority. [First, the] incorporation of the right recognized in Heller would amount to a significant incursion on a traditional and important area of state concern, altering the constitutional relationship between the States and the Federal Government. [Second, determining] the constitutionality of a particular state gun law requires finding answers to complex empirically based questions of a kind that legislatures are better able than courts to make. [Third, the] ability of States to reflect local preferences and conditions—both key virtues of federalism—here has particular importance. The incidence of gun ownership varies substantially as between crowded cities and uncongested rural communities, as well as among the different geographic regions of the country. [The] nature of gun violence also varies as between rural communities and cities. [Fourth,] incorporation of any right removes decisions from the democratic process."

After concluding that all of these factors militated against incorporation, Justice Breyer ended by emphasizing that history too was an equivocal source of support for incorporation: "Although the majority does not discuss 20th-or 21st-century evidence concerning the Second Amendment at any length, I think that it is essential to consider the recent history of the right to bear arms for private self-defense when considering whether the right is 'fundamental.' [By] the end of the 20th century, in every State and many local communities, highly detailed and complicated regulatory schemes governed (and continue to govern) nearly every aspect of firearm ownership. [And] state courts in States with constitutions that provide gun rights have almost uniformly interpreted those rights as providing protection only against unreasonable regulation of guns. [Ambiguous] history cannot show that the Fourteenth Amendment incorporates a private right of self-defense against the States."

CHAPTER 11

FREEDOM OF SPEECH—WHY GOVERNMENT RESTRICTS SPEECH—UNPROTECTED AND LESS PROTECTED EXPRESSION

SECTION 5.   SEXUALLY EXPLICIT EXPRESSION

Page 885. Add after note 4:

5. *Extending Ferber to "crush videos" or other depictions of cruelty to animals?* The Court has not designated any category of speech "unprotected" since Ferber placed child pornography outside the reach of the First Amendment. Are there other categories of speech so presumptively injurious and lacking in social value that they may likewise be deemed unprotected? Is the Chaplinsky list open to new entrants? In UNITED STATES v. STEVENS, ___ U.S. ___, 130 S.Ct. 1577 (2010), the Supreme Court was asked to consider whether certain portrayals of cruelty toward animals merited exclusion from First Amendment protection. The case involved a facial challenge to 18 U.S.C. § 48, which criminalizes the commercial creation, sale, or possession of any visual or auditory depiction "in which a living animal is intentionally maimed, mutilated, tortured, wounded, or killed," if that conduct violates federal or state law where "the creation, sale, or possession takes place," unless the depiction has "serious religious, political, scientific, educational, journalistic, historical, or artistic value." While the legislative history focused primarily on "crush videos," which show torture and killing of helpless animals to appeal to a sexual fetish, the statute's text was not limited to such videos. Stevens challenged his indictment for distributing videos of dogfighting, which is unlawful in all 50 States and the District of Columbia.

Writing for an 8–1 majority from which only Justice Alito dissented, Chief Justice ROBERTS declined to treat "depictions of animal cruelty, as a class, [as] categorically unprotected by the First Amendment," and thus declined to add such speech to the " 'well-defined and narrowly limited classes of speech, the prevention and punishment of which have never been thought to raise any Constitutional problem.' Chaplinsky v. New Hampshire." The Chief Justice rejected the government's argument that First Amendment protection should be determined by " 'categorical balancing of the value of the speech against its societal costs.' " He wrote: "As a free-floating test for First Amendment coverage, that sentence is startling and dangerous. The First Amendment's guarantee of free speech does not extend only to categories of speech that survive an ad hoc balancing of relative social costs and benefits. The First Amendment itself reflects a judgment by the American people that the benefits of its restrictions on the Government outweigh the costs. Our Constitution forecloses any attempt to revise that judgment simply on the basis that some speech is not worth it. [When] we have identified categories of speech as fully outside the protection of the First Amendment, it has not been on the basis of a simple cost-benefit analysis. In Ferber, for example, we classified child pornography as such a category [because the] market for child pornography was 'intrinsically related' to the underlying abuse, and was therefore 'an integral part of the production of such materials, an activity illegal throughout the Nation.' [Our] decisions in Ferber and other cases cannot be taken as establishing a freewheeling authority to declare new categories of speech outside the scope of the First Amendment." Without deciding whether "whether a statute limited to crush videos or other depictions of extreme animal cruelty would be constitutional," the majority opinion found the statute substantially overbroad and thus facially invalid. For the overbreadth portion of the opinion, see p. 21 below.

In a solo dissent, Justice ALITO disagreed with the Court's overbreadth ruling and stated that he would have found crush videos unprotected under the reasoning in Ferber: "The First Amendment protects freedom of speech, but it most certainly does not protect violent criminal conduct, even if engaged in for expressive purposes. Crush videos [record] the commission of violent criminal acts, and it appears that these crimes are committed for the sole purpose of creating the videos. [Congress] was presented with compelling evidence that the only way of preventing these crimes was to target the sale of the videos. Under these circumstances, I cannot believe that the First Amendment commands Congress to step aside and allow the underlying crimes to continue. [The] most relevant of our prior decisions is Ferber. [The] Court there held that child pornography is not protected speech, and I believe that Ferber's reasoning dictates a similar conclusion here." Justice Alito observed that, here as in Ferber, "the conduct depicted in crush videos is criminal in every State and the District of Columbia," "the criminal acts shown in crush videos cannot be prevented without targeting the conduct prohibited by § 48—the creation, sale, and possession for sale of depictions of animal torture," and "the harm caused by the underlying crimes vastly outweighs any minimal value that the depictions might conceivably be thought to possess." He would have extended the same reasoning to "depictions of brutal animal fights," which, "like crush videos, record the actual commission of a crime involving deadly violence," "cannot be effectively controlled without targeting the videos," and "have by definition no appreciable social value" given the exemption for those depictions "with a modicum of social value."

CHAPTER 12

FREEDOM OF SPEECH—HOW GOVERNMENT RESTRICTS SPEECH— MODES OF ABRIDGMENT AND STANDARDS OF REVIEW

SECTION 1. THE DISTINCTION BETWEEN CONTENT-BASED AND CONTENT-NEUTRAL REGULATIONS

Page 973. Add after note 4:

5. *Material support to terrorism through speech activities: conduct or speech?* What sort of scrutiny should be applied to a statute that prohibits material support to designated foreign terrorist organizations, as applied to speech activities by such organizations that are themselves related to lawful, nonviolent objectives? In HOLDER v. HUMANITARIAN LAW PROJECT, ___ U.S. ___, 130 S.Ct. 2705 (2010), several organizations that had been designated foreign terrorist organizations by the Secretary of State challenged a federal statute, 18 U.S.C. § 2339B(a)(1), that criminalizes "knowingly provid[ing] material support or resources to a foreign terrorist organization," as applied to certain of their speech activities. The Court declined to apply O'Brien review, as the government urged, but nonetheless upheld, under apparent strict scrutiny, the challenged applications of the statute. "Material support" under the statute is defined to include "training," "expert advice or assistance," "service," and "personnel." The challengers—supporters of the Partiya Karkeran Kurdistan (PKK), which aims to establish an independent state for Kurds in Turkey, and the Liberation Tigers of Tamil Eelam (LTTE), which seeks the same for Tamils in Sri Lanka—sought a determination that these provisions of the statute could not constitutionally apply to the organizations' lawful, nonviolent activities, including training PKK members to use international law to resolve disputes peacefully and to petition the United Nations for relief, and engaging in political advocacy on behalf of Kurds and Tamils.

Chief Justice ROBERTS wrote for the Court, joined by Justices Stevens, Scalia, Kennedy, Thomas and Alito. After rejecting a Fifth Amendment vagueness challenge, the Chief Justice turned to the relevant standard of First Amendment scrutiny, and rejected both the challengers' and the government's positions. Finding that the "statute is carefully drawn to cover only a narrow category of speech to, under the direction of, or in coordination with foreign groups that the speaker knows to be terrorist organizations," he rejected the challengers' claims that the statute burdened their pure political speech. At the same time, he rejected the government's argument that the statute was subject merely to O'Brien review as a regulation of conduct: "The law here may be described as directed at conduct, as the law in Cohen was directed at breaches of the peace, but as applied to plaintiffs the conduct triggering coverage under the statute consists of communicating a message." Accordingly, he wrote, " 'we are outside of O'Brien's test, and we must [apply] a more demanding standard.' "

Applying that standard, he continued: "The First Amendment issue before us is [whether] the Government may prohibit [material] support to the PKK and LTTE in the form of speech. Everyone agrees that the Government's interest in combating terrorism is an urgent objective of the highest order. Plaintiffs' complaint is that the ban on material support, applied to what they wish to do, is not 'necessary to further that interest' [because] their support will advance only the legitimate activities of the designated terrorist organizations, not their terrorism. Whether foreign terrorist organizations meaningfully segregate support of their legitimate activities from support of terrorism is an empirical question. [Material] support meant to 'promot[e] peaceable, lawful conduct' can further terrorism by foreign groups in multiple ways. 'Material support' is a valuable resource by definition. Such support frees up other resources within the organization that may be put to violent ends. It also importantly helps lend legitimacy to foreign terrorist groups—legitimacy that makes it easier for those groups to persist, to recruit members, and to raise funds—all of which facilitate more terrorist attacks. [Money] is fungible, and [there] is evidence that the PKK and the LTTE [have] not 'respected the line between humanitarian and violent activities.' "

The Chief Justice suggested that the national security context made it appropriate to accord "significant weight" to the views of the executive branch, and noted that there was evidence in the record that " 'the U.S. government agencies charged with combating terrorism strongly suppor[t]' Congress's finding that all contributions to foreign terrorist organizations further their terrorism." He concluded: "Given the sensitive interests in national security and foreign affairs at stake, the political branches have adequately substantiated their determination that, to serve the Government's interest in preventing terrorism, it was necessary to prohibit providing material support in the form of training, expert advice, personnel, and services to foreign terrorist groups, even if the supporters meant to promote only the groups' nonviolent ends." The majority opinion found no basis to invalidate the statute as applied to the challengers' particular proposed activities.

Justice BREYER dissented, joined by Justices Ginsburg and Sotomayor: "[T]he Government has not made the strong showing necessary to justify under the First Amendment the criminal prosecution of those who engage in these activities. All the activities involve the communication and advocacy of political ideas and lawful means of achieving political ends. [Where,] as here, a statute applies criminal penalties and at least arguably does so on the basis of content-based distinctions, I should think we would scrutinize the statute and justifications 'strictly'—to determine whether the prohibition is justified by a 'compelling' need that cannot be 'less restrictively' accommodated. [The] Government does identify a compelling countervailing interest, namely, the interest in protecting the security of the United States and its nationals from the threats that foreign terrorist organizations pose by denying those organizations financial and other fungible resources. I do not dispute the importance of this interest. But I do dispute whether the interest can justify the statute's criminal prohibition." The dissent questioned the strength of the government's evidence that "the plaintiffs' political-advocacy-related activities might actually be 'fungible' and therefore capable of being diverted to terrorist use," and expressed skepticism toward the claim that lawful speech may be stopped lest it "bolster" terrorism, given that "the Government allows much other 'speech' legitimating' a terrorist group."

To avoid these serious constitutional difficulties, Justice Breyer would have construed the statute "as criminalizing First–Amendment-protected pure speech and association only when the defendant knows or intends that those activities will assist the organization's unlawful terrorist actions. Under this reading, the Government would have to show, at a minimum, that such defendants provided support that they knew was significantly likely to help the organization pursue its unlawful terrorist aims. [This] reading of the statute protects those who engage in pure speech and association ordinarily protected by the First Amendment. But it does not protect that activity where a defendant purposefully intends it to help terrorism or where a defendant knows (or willfully blinds himself to the fact) that the activity is significantly likely to assist terrorism." The dissent would have remanded for consideration of whether the challengers' proposed activities were proscribable under this standard.

SECTION 2.   GOVERNMENT'S POWER TO LIMIT SPEECH IN ITS CAPACITY AS LANDLORD, EDUCATOR, EMPLOYER AND PATRON

Page 1050. Add after note 10:

11. *Student organization membership at a public law school.* Do "limited public forum" principles extend to the setting of membership in public university student organizations? In CHRISTIAN LEGAL SOCIETY CHAPTER OF UNIV. OF CALIFORNIA HASTINGS COLLEGE OF LAW v. MARTINEZ, ___ U.S. ___, 130 S.Ct. 2971 (2010), a public law school within the University of California system established a "Registered Student Organization (RSO)" program that conferred the use of school funds, facilities, and the law school's name and logo on condition that RSOs allow "all comers" to participate, become members or seek leadership positions, regardless of their status or beliefs. The parties jointly stipulated in the lower courts that the policy was universally applied to all groups: " 'Hastings requires that registered student organizations allow *any* student to participate, become a member, or seek leadership positions in the organization, regardless of [her] status or beliefs. Thus, for example, the Hastings Democratic Caucus cannot bar students holding Republican political beliefs from becoming members or seeking leadership positions in the organization.' " Under this policy, Hastings declined to grant RSO status to a chapter of the Christian Legal Society (CLS) on the ground that, by requiring members and officers to sign onto a "Statement of Faith" and renounce "unrepentant homosexual conduct," it excluded students based on religion and sexual orientation in violation of the all-comers policy.

CLS challenged this denial, claiming that application of the all-comers policy violated its rights to freedom of speech and association.

The Supreme Court rejected the First Amendment challenge by a closely divided 5–4 vote. Justice GINSBURG wrote for the majority, joined by Justices Stevens, Kennedy, Breyer and Sotomayor. Crucial to her decision was the premise that "Hastings, through its RSO program, [had] established a limited public forum." She explained: "In diverse contexts, our decisions have distinguished between policies that require action and those that withhold benefits. Application of the less-restrictive limited-public-forum analysis better accounts for the fact that Hastings, through its RSO program, is dangling the carrot of subsidy, not wielding the stick of prohibition." And she found limited-public-forum principles equally dispositive of CLS's free speech and expressive-association claims.

Justice Ginsburg reiterated the standard of scrutiny governing such a forum: "Recognizing a State's right to preserve the property under its control for the use to which it is lawfully dedicated, the Court has permitted restrictions on access to a limited public forum, like the RSO program here, with this key caveat: Any access barrier must be reasonable and viewpoint neutral." Applying that standard, she first considered "whether Hastings' policy is reasonable taking into account the RSO forum's function and 'all the surrounding circumstances,'" and answered that question in the affirmative: "[A] college's commission—and its concomitant license to choose among pedagogical approaches—is not confined to the classroom, for extracurricular programs are, today, essential parts of the educational process. [First,] the open-access policy 'ensures that the leadership, educational, and social opportunities afforded by [RSOs] are available to all students.' [Second,] the all-comers requirement helps Hastings police the written terms of its Nondiscrimination Policy without inquiring into an RSO's motivation for membership restrictions. [Third,] the Law School reasonably adheres to the view that an all-comers policy, to the extent it brings together individuals with diverse backgrounds and beliefs, 'encourages tolerance, cooperation, and learning among students.' [These] several justifications [are] surely reasonable in light of the RSO forum's purposes."

Justice Ginsburg next "consider[ed] whether Hastings' all-comers policy is viewpoint neutral," and again answered affirmatively: "In contrast to [Widmar and Rosenberger], in which universities singled out organizations for disfavored treatment because of their points of view, Hastings' all-comers requirement draws no distinction between groups based on their message or perspective. An all-comers condition on access to RSO status, in short, is textbook viewpoint neutral." The majority opinion rejected CLS's argument that the policy is viewpoint-discriminatory in effect because " 'it systematically and predictably burdens most heavily those groups whose viewpoints are out of favor with the campus mainstream,' " finding that such a "differential impact" did not render the policy nonneutral. Justice Ginsburg concluded: "Finding Hastings' open-access condition on RSO status reasonable and viewpoint neutral, we reject CLS' free-speech and expressive-association claims."

Justice STEVENS, joined by Justice Kennedy, concurred to emphasize that "[i]t is critical, in evaluating CLS's challenge [to] keep in mind that an RSO program is a limited forum—the boundaries of which may be delimited by the proprietor. When a religious association, or a secular association, operates in a wholly public setting, it must be allowed broad freedom to control its membership and its message, even if its decisions cause offense to outsiders. [But] the CLS chapter that brought this lawsuit does not want to be just a Christian group; it aspires to be a recognized student organization. The Hastings College of Law is not a legislature. And no state actor has demanded that anyone do anything outside the confines of a discrete, voluntary academic program. [The] RSO forum is [not] an open commons that Hastings happens to maintain. It is a mechanism through which Hastings confers certain benefits and pursues certain aspects of its educational mission. [CLS] excludes students who will not sign its Statement of Faith or who engage in 'unrepentant homosexual conduct.' Other groups may exclude or mistreat Jews, blacks, and women—or those who do not share their contempt for Jews, blacks, and women. A free society must tolerate such groups. It need not subsidize them, give them its official imprimatur, or grant them equal access to law school facilities."

Justice KENNEDY filed a concurrence emphasizing the case's differences from Rosenberger v. Rector (1995; 17th ed. p. 1093): "[H]ere the school policy in question is not content based either in its formulation or evident purpose; and were it shown to be otherwise, the case likely should have a different outcome. Here, the policy applies equally to all groups and views. And, given the stipulation of the parties, there is no basis for an allegation that the design or purpose of the rule was, by subterfuge, to discriminate based on viewpoint."

Justice ALITO dissented, joined by Chief Justice Roberts and Justices Scalia and Thomas. The dissent began by vigorously disputing that the stipulation setting forth the all-comers policy truly captured the policy Hastings had applied, arguing that the policy was a pretextual substitute for a prior Nondiscrimination Policy that in practice discriminated against student groups organized around religious viewpoints. The dissent next argued that the case should have been controlled by Healy v. James, 408 U.S. 169 (1972), which invalidated a public college's refusal to recognize a student chapter of Students for a Democratic Society (SDS) because it would not renounce violence.

Reaching the limited-public-forum principles central to the majority opinion, Justice Alito argued that Hastings' application of its policy is impermissible even if the stipulated all-comers policy were deemed the operative policy and the RSO program were deemed a limited public forum: "Taken as a whole, the regulations plainly contemplate the creation of a forum within which Hastings students are free to form and obtain registration of essentially the same broad range of private groups that nonstudents may form off campus. [The] way in which the RSO forum actually developed corroborates this design. [Hastings] had more than 60 RSOs in 2004–2005, each with its own independently devised purpose. Some addressed serious social issues; others—for example, the wine appreciation and ultimate Frisbee clubs—were simply recreational. Some organizations focused on a subject but did not claim to promote a particular viewpoint on that subject (for example, the Association of Communications, Sports & Entertainment Law); others were defined, not by subject, but by viewpoint. The forum did not have a single Party Politics Club; rather, it featured both the Hastings Democratic Caucus and the Hastings Republicans. There was no Reproductive Issues Club; the forum included separate pro-choice and pro-life organizations. Students did not see fit to create a Monotheistic

Religions Club, but they have formed the Hastings Jewish Law Students Association and the Hastings Association of Muslim Law Students. In short, the RSO forum, true to its design, has allowed Hastings students to replicate on campus a broad array of private, independent, noncommercial organizations that is very similar to those that nonstudents have formed in the outside world. The accept-all-comers policy is antithetical to the design of the RSO forum for the same reason that a state-imposed accept-all-comers policy would violate the First Amendment rights of private groups if applied off campus."

SECTION 3.   IMPERMISSIBLE METHODS OF RESTRICTING SPEECH: OVERBREADTH, VAGUENESS AND PRIOR RESTRAINT

Page 1116. Add to end of note 7:

In UNITED STATES v. STEVENS, ___ U.S. ___, 130 S.Ct. 1577 (2010), the Court facially invalidated, as overbroad, 18 U.S.C. § 48, which criminalizes the commercial creation, sale, or possession of any visual or auditory depiction "in which a living animal is intentionally maimed, mutilated, tortured, wounded, or killed," if that conduct violates federal or state law where "the creation, sale, or possession takes place," unless the depiction has "serious religious, political, scientific, educational, journalistic, historical, or artistic value." Without deciding whether depictions of extreme animal cruelty might be categorically prohibited by a narrower law, the Court, in a 8–1 opinion by Chief Justice ROBERTS, held the statute invalid as overbroad because " 'a substantial number of its applications are unconstitutional, judged in relation to the statute's plainly legitimate sweep.' "

In explicating the overbreadth basis for the ruling, the Chief Justice wrote: "We read § 48 to create a criminal prohibition of alarming breadth. [The] text of the statute's ban on a 'depiction of animal cruelty' nowhere requires that the depicted conduct be cruel. [What] is more, the application of § 48 to depictions of illegal conduct extends to conduct that is illegal in only a single jurisdiction. [Views] about cruelty to animals and regulations having no connection to cruelty vary widely from place to place. In the District of Columbia, for example, all hunting is unlawful. Other jurisdictions permit or encourage hunting, and there is an enormous national market for hunting-related depictions in which a living animal is intentionally killed." The Chief Justice rejected the government's argument that the statute was sufficiently narrowed by its exemption for "any depiction that has serious religious, political, scientific, educational, journalistic, historical, or artistic value." And he denied that Miller v. California, on which the "serious value" exception was modeled, had held "that serious value could be used as a general precondition to protecting other types of speech." Noting that "the markets for crush videos and dogfighting depictions [are] dwarfed by the market for other depictions, such as hunting magazines and videos," covered by § 48, the Chief Justice concluded that "the presumptively impermissible applications of § 48 (properly construed) far outnumber any permissible ones," and thus that the statute was facially invalid for overbreadth.

The sole dissenter, Justice ALITO, disputed the Court's conclusion that § 48 bans a substantial quantity of protected speech. Noting that overbreadth analysis should focus on "a statute's application to real-world conduct, not fanciful hypotheticals," he denied that § 48 even applies to the depictions of hunting on which the majority focused, as hunting is generally legal in all 50 states and any exceptions are not based on the prevention of animal cruelty. He also found the scope of other possible protected speech reached by the statute too trivial to warrant invalidation for substantial overbreadth, noting that "nothing in the record suggests that any one has ever created, sold, or possessed for sale a depiction of the slaughter of food animals or of the docking of the tails of dairy cows that would not easily qualify under the exception" for depictions with serious value.

For portions of the decision declining to denominate depictions of animal cruelty a new, unprotected category of speech, see p. 14 above.

CHAPTER 13

RIGHTS ANCILLARY TO FREEDOM OF SPEECH

SECTION 1. COMPELLED SPEECH: THE RIGHT *NOT* TO SPEAK

Page 1145. Add to end of note 3:

If the First Amendment as interpreted in McIntyre v. Ohio Elections Commission protects the right to leaflet anonymously, may one who signs a petition to place a referendum on the ballot also claim a right to anonymity? In DOE v. REED, ___ U.S. ___, 130 S.Ct. 2811 (2010), the Supreme Court rebuffed such a claim, upholding against First Amendment challenge a requirement of Washington's Public Records Act (PRA) that the names and addresses of those who sign referendum ballot petitions be publicly disclosed. The challenge was brought by supporters of a petition challenging a state law extending certain benefits to same-sex couples.

Writing for an 8–1 majority joined by all but Justice Thomas, Chief Justice ROBERTS explained: "The compelled disclosure of signatory information on referendum petitions is subject to review under the First Amendment. An individual expresses a view on a political matter when he signs a petition under Washington's referendum procedure. In most cases, the individual's signature will express the view that the law subject to the petition should be overturned. [But] that is not to say that the electoral context is irrelevant to the nature of our First Amendment review. [First] Amendment challenges to disclosure requirements in the electoral context [are subject to] 'exacting scrutiny,' which 'requires a "substantial relation" between the disclosure requirement and a "sufficiently important" governmental interest.'" Under that standard, the Chief Justice found disclosure of petition information substantially related to an important interest in "preserving the integrity of the electoral process by combating fraud, detecting invalid signatures, and fostering government transparency and accountability." He accordingly did not reach or resolve the question whether the State had a constitutionally sufficient interest in "providing information to the electorate about who supports the petition."

As the Chief Justice noted, the challengers objected that, "once on the Internet, the petition signers' names and addresses 'can be combined with publicly available phone numbers and maps,' in what will effectively become a blueprint for harassment and intimidation. To support their claim that they will be subject to reprisals, plaintiffs cite examples from the history of a similar proposition in California [i.e., Proposition 8, overturning a decision of the California Supreme Court upholding a constitutional right to gay marriage]." But stating that "typical referendum petitions 'concern tax policy, revenue, budget, or other state law issues,'" he found "no reason to assume that any burdens imposed by disclosure of typical referendum petitions would be remotely like the burdens plaintiffs fear in this case." He concluded: "[W]e must reject plaintiffs' broad challenge to the PRA. In doing so, we note [that] upholding the law against a broad-based challenge does not foreclose a litigant's success in a narrower one" if disclosure could be shown to pose a specific danger of threats, reprisal or harassment.

Justice ALITO concurred, emphasizing the need for potential petition signators to be able to obtain such as-applied exemptions "quickly and well in advance of speaking" and "without clearing a high evidentiary hurdle." He suggested that the petitioners in this case would have a strong argument for an as-applied exemption on remand, given evidence of "widespread harassment and intimidation suffered by supporters of California's Proposition 8." He suggested that any "informational" interest in disclosure attenuates upon proof of risk of harassment, and expressed skepticism about the need for disclosure to prevent electoral fraud, noting that California, which "has had more initiatives on the ballot than any other State save Oregon, [explicitly] protects the privacy of initiative and referendum signatories."

Justice SOTOMAYOR, joined by Justices Stevens and Ginsburg, filed a concurrence emphasizing that the State has strong interests in the integrity of the ballot process and that "the burden of public disclosure on speech and associational rights [is] minimal in this context [as] the process of legislating by referendum is inherently public." She suggested that "any party attempting to challenge particular applications of the State's regulations will bear a heavy burden," and that as-applied exceptions should be available only "when a State selectively applies a facially neutral petition disclosure rule in a manner that discriminates based on the content of referenda or the viewpoint of petition signers, or in the rare circumstance in which disclosure poses a reasonable probability of serious and widespread harassment that the State is unwilling or unable to control."

Justice STEVENS, joined by Justice Breyer, concurred in part and in the judgment, stating that this was "not a hard case" and emphasizing that, unlike in McIntyre, the PRA does not "require that any person signing a petition disclose or say anything." Like Justice Sotomayor, he suggested that as-applied challenges to petition disclosure requirements should be sparingly granted: "For an as-applied challenge to a law such as the PRA to succeed, there would have to be a significant threat of harassment directed at those who sign the petition that cannot be mitigated by law enforcement measures. [Debates] about tax policy and regulation of private property can become just as heated as debates about domestic partnerships. And as a general matter, it is very difficult to show that by later disclosing the names of petition signatories, individuals will be less willing to sign petitions. [I] would demand strong evidence before concluding that an indirect and speculative chain of events imposes a substantial burden on speech."

Justice SCALIA concurred only in the judgment, expressing "doubt whether signing a petition that has the effect of suspending a law fits within 'the freedom of speech' at all" and arguing that "[w]e should not repeat and extend the mistake of McIntyre v. Ohio Elections Comm'n." He would forego "judicial interest-balancing" in this context and hold that "[o]ur Nation's longstanding traditions of legislating and voting in public refute the claim that the First

Amendment accords a right to anonymity in the performance of an act with governmental effect." He continued: "When a Washington voter signs a referendum petition subject to the PRA, he is acting as a legislator. [The] exercise of lawmaking power in the United States has traditionally been public. [Voting] was public until 1888 when the States began to adopt the Australian secret ballot. [The] long history of public legislating and voting contradicts plaintiffs' claim that disclosure of petition signatures having legislative effect violates the First Amendment." As to the petitioners' claimed fears of harassment, Justice Scalia replied: "There are laws against threats and intimidation; and harsh criticism, short of unlawful action, is a price our people have traditionally been willing to pay for self-governance. Requiring people to stand up in public for their political acts fosters civic courage, without which democracy is doomed."

Justice THOMAS filed the lone dissent. He would have found the PRA's compelled disclosure requirement unconstitutional because it "severely burdens [and] chills citizen participation in the referendum process" and "there will always be a less restrictive means by which Washington can vindicate its stated interest in preserving the integrity of its referendum process." He explained: "[U]nlike the Court, I read our precedents to require application of strict scrutiny to laws that compel disclosure of protected First Amendment association," meaning that "a disclosure requirement passes constitutional muster only if it is [the] least restrictive means to serve a compelling state interest." Even if the State has a compelling interest in electoral integrity, he argued, it does not need to use the "blunderbuss" approach of public disclosure of referendum signers' names and addresses: it "could put the names and addresses of referendum signers into [an] electronic database that state employees could search without subjecting the name and address of each signer to wholesale public disclosure," "could create a Web site, linked to the electronic referendum database, where a voter concerned that his name had been fraudulently signed could conduct a search using his unique identifier to ensure that his name was absent from the database," or could otherwise enforce existing laws against fraud. And, citing McIntyre, he found constitutionally insufficient any state " 'interest in providing the electorate with relevant information.' " Finding as-applied challenges too time-consuming and cumbersome to protect the speech interests at stake, he would have invalidated the PRA's disclosure requirement on its face.

†